THE LEARNER'S POCKETBOOK

By Paul Hayden

Drawings by Phil Hailstone

"Should prove very useful to those studying for exams, also those with an interest in how we learn. I like the idea of being able to 'dip into' different areas as and when needed."
Hazel Garvey, Technical and Training Manager, Joint Monitoring Unit, The Institute of Chartered Accountants

"Inspiring, practical and enjoyable; a must for all learners, their trainers and teachers. A number of new elements, which I find exciting."
Joe Culkin, Head of Learning and Development, Raychem Ltd

CONTENTS

FOREWORD BY TONY BUZAN

As we approach rapidly the 21st Century, it is becoming increasingly apparent that it will become known as the 'Century of the Brain'.

Global business leaders are crying out for more Brainpower, the development of Intellectual Capital, and investment in the most powerful currency in the world - the currency of Intelligence.

This growing development of the awareness *by* intelligence *of* intelligence, and the fact that this quality is not only multiple but can be nurtured and grown, is one of the great beacons of hope for the future of our race. When Humankind becomes truly mentally literate - understanding both the alphabet of the neuro physiology of the brain and the alphabet of its behaviour, including memory, creativity, thinking, reading and learning - the world will, in all probability, approach the utopia which for many millennia has been the dream of so many different societies.

Paul Hayden's delightful **The Learner's Pocketbook** is a considered and intelligent introduction to this intriguing field, and will start the 'learner of learning' off in the right direction - on a journey that will provide immeasurable satisfactions and reward.

'The only educated
man is the one
who has learned
how to learn'

Arthur C. Clarke

HOW TO USE THIS BOOK

Before reading any further

- List key words/headings of existing knowledge on how to learn

- Write down the questions you want this book to answer

- Write down the benefits to you of learning how to learn

Now - browse **quickly** through the book looking at 'contents', pictures, diagrams, headings, subjects.

If it will not answer your questions or give you the benefits you seek:
DO NOT READ THIS BOOK

HOW TO USE THIS BOOK

If it **will** answer your questions and give you those benefits:

- Browse more slowly, taking in the same as before but also the organisation and structure of the book

- When you start to read 'properly' consider carefully where you read and for how long

- As you read - mark pages, make notes, colour in diagrams, complete exercises and use what you learn as you read

- Skip tricky text and refer back to it later

Finished reading - summarise key points. Apply what you have learned - otherwise you have not learned.

Celebrate your success and continue to learn.

BRAIN POWER

NEURONS

- The brain has 10 - 15 billion neurons (over twice the number of people in the world)

- The number of neurons does not determine intelligence; the number of **connections** does

- There are at least 10 trillion (10,000,000,000,000) connections, called synapses

- A synapse is the point where the axon of one neuron connects with the dendrite of another

NEURONS

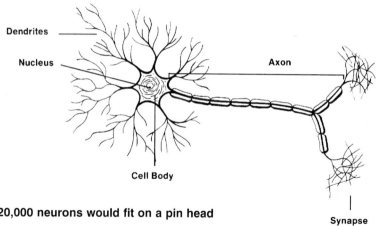

Dendrites

Nucleus

Axon

Cell Body

Synapse

20,000 neurons would fit on a pin head

BRAIN POWER

THREE BRAINS

Neocortex ('cortex')
Comprises 2 sided cerebrum, left and right brain
Back processes visual data
Side processes auditory data
Centre strip processes data from touch
Controls intellectual processes - talking, seeing, hearing, reasoning, thinking

Mammalian brain ('limbic system')
Contains hypothalamus, pituitary gland and hippo campus
Plays a vital role in long term memory
Controls emotion, sexuality, health, immune system, sleep

Reptilian brain ('brain stem')
Stems from the spinal column
Controls basic instincts - breathing, heart rate, sense of territory

THREE BRAINS

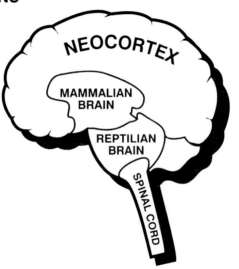

NEOCORTEX

MAMMALIAN BRAIN

REPTILIAN BRAIN

SPINAL CORD

LEFT & RIGHT BRAIN

'L' Logical brain

'R' aRtistic brain

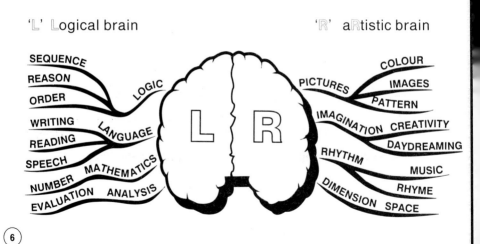

LEFT & RIGHT BRAIN

Combining the **L**eft and **R**ight brain increases your

L ea R ning

For example:

Learning a song:

- Left brain processes the words
- Right brain processes the music

combine both by singing

Learning with Mind Maps:

- Left brain processes words and order
- Right brain processes colour and images

combine both in a Mind Map

BRAIN POWER

VITAL STATISTICS

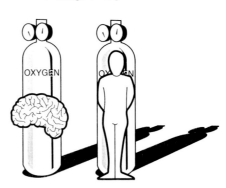

- Average adult brain weighs 3 lbs (1.4 kg) =

  1½ bags of sugar

- The brain uses 25% of the body's oxygen and blood supply, but is only 3% of bodyweight

LEARNING THEORY

THE LEARNING CURVE

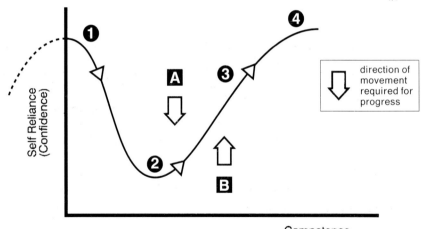

LEARNING THEORY

THE LEARNING CURVE

1 **Unconscious incompetent** Your confidence exceeds your ability, you are not knowledgeable/skilful
2 **Conscious incompetent** Your confidence drops as you realise your ability is limited
3 **Conscious competent** Your confidence increases with your ability, you have to concentrate on what you know/do
4 **Unconscious competent** Your confidence and ability have peaked, you no longer have to concentrate on what you know/do; this is the start of the next learning curve

In different areas of your life you will be at different stages on different learning curves.

In order to learn, you must be on the curve, so you can move forward.

At [A] confidence exceeds ability - a drop in confidence is needed to move forward.

At [B] ability exceeds confidence - a boost in confidence is needed to move forward.

THE FOUR STAGES OF LEARNING

Reasoning
- Focus your mind on why you are learning
- Get in a positive frame of mind

Planning
- Break the bulk of your learning down into manageable chunks
- Plan your time and environment

Committing
- Commit yourself to learn
- Put knowledge into your brain for future use

Reflecting
- Prove to yourself you know
- Get better, for future learning

REASONING

FOCUS THE MIND

'Why am I learning?' - If you do not know, you will not learn.

Remember

ie: Do not make your focus passing an exam or achieving a qualification. Focus on what that qualification gives you or will do for you.

REASONING

FOCUS THE MIND

Prepare your mind for learning:

Use **POSITIVE** affirmations
{ 'I enjoy learning'
{ 'I learn and remember easily'
{ 'I am a confident learner', etc

Visualise what success will feel and look like - use positive past experiences.

Positive experiences are more easily remembered, make whatever you learn easier to remember.

WIIFM

Use this page to record what you will gain from learning how to learn.

PLANNING

CREATING TIME

We all have the same resource - 86,400 seconds in a 24 hour day; how you invest yours is important.

Create time for learning, eg:

- Get up $\frac{1}{2}$ hour earlier or go to bed $\frac{1}{2}$ hour later (or both)
- Rearrange other activities to free up chunks of time
- Sacrifice other activities, remember WIIFM
- Switch off the TV when the programme you want to watch finishes
- Integrate study with other areas of your life
- Sacrifice lunch breaks occasionally, grab a sandwich (do not skip lunch, just the break)
- Use travel time on buses and trains
- Carry notes/books, etc, to study during downtime, eg: queuing

STRUCTURE YOUR LEARNING

Salami Method

Does not look appealing until

you slice it up

Break your learning down into manageable pieces; it makes it easier to swallow.

Backward Thinking

- Start with the end in mind
- Work back from your target/deadline date
- Spread out your 'slices'
- Easy to focus on what needs to be done daily

LEARNING PLAN

- Use your diary to plan your learning

- Plan days off as a reward

- Commit to learning when those days arrive and enjoy the days off - do not overdo it

You can use this learning plan, photocopy it as many times as necessary.

Experiment with various times of the day, if possible, to see when you learn best.

LEARNING PLAN

Subject _____

Day	Date	0	1	2	3	4	5	6	7	8	9	10	11	12	13	14	15	16	17	18	19	20	21	22	23
Sun																									
Mon																									
Tue																									
Wed																									
Thu																									
Fri																									
Sat																									

MIND & BODY
DIET - VITAMINS

Vitamin A - Aids vision, found in fats and oils

B Vitamins - Keep you mentally alert, found in wholegrains, seeds, lentils, yeast, nuts, eggs and milk products
Vitamin B5 and B6 are particularly important for memory, also found in fish and chicken
Vitamin B3 is essential for proper brain functioning
Vitamin B12 is essential for the production of red blood cells, which carry oxygen, and is found in animal products such as meat, milk and eggs
Vegetarians may need to take extra as it is scarce in their diet

Vitamin C - Anti-oxidant, protects other vitamins from destruction, found in fresh fruit and vegetables

Vitamin E - Increases cell oxygenisation, found in wholegrains, whole wheat and sunflower seed oil

(22) **N.B.** Consult your GP before taking vitamin supplements.

PLANNING

MIND & BODY

DIET - GENERAL

Too much sugar, starch, caffeine, alcohol and other unnecessary drugs lead to mental dullness.

Keep a well balanced diet.

As diet has deteriorated, more and more people are suffering from mental illness, most commonly anxiety and depression.

Glucose generates the 20/25 watts[*] of electricity that enables the brain to function. The brain uses two thirds of the body's glucose. Keep a steady supply in your blood stream, do not skip meals, especially breakfast.

You would not put the wrong fuel into a high performance sports car, do not put the wrong fuel in your body and mind.

[*] Source - How to Boost Your Brain Power - Roger B Yepsen, Jnr, Thorsons

MIND & BODY

RELAXATION

Energy for learning is released through relaxation. Before learning, bring about a calm and positive mood.

Simple relaxation exercises:

With your eyes closed, sit and:
- Listen to relaxing music
- Tense and relax each muscle in turn, starting with your feet and working up your body
- Imagine walking down a flight of stairs; after each step, exhale and say 'I am even more relaxed now'

These exercises have a double effect as they also stimulate both sides of the brain in preparation for learning.

MIND & BODY
EXERCISE

- Exercise regularly to clear the arteries and oxygenate the blood

Remember 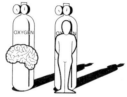 Brain uses 25% of body's oxygen and blood supply

- Controlled rhythmic breathing results in greater brain oxidation

- Use what exercise works best for you, but remember:
  regular rest is also necessary for the brain to function fully

'Mens sana in corpore sano'
(A healthy mind in a healthy body)

PLANNING

ENVIRONMENT

Workspace

- Should be inviting and encourage study
- Remove all distractions
- Ensure everything you need is to hand: books, pens, glasses, etc
- Display posters and Mind Maps to stimulate your mind

Table/Desk

- Navel height, with as much space as necessary
- Do not cramp yourself

Chair

- Comfortable and straight backed
- High enough so your feet are flat on the floor and thighs parallel to the ground
- Good posture increases supply of blood to the brain

ENVIRONMENT

Temperature

- Not too warm otherwise you relax

Light

- Natural light is best - sit by a window
- Standard bulb is better than fluorescent

Air

- Fresh air, have the window nearest you open
- Oxygen is essential for the brain to function; the cleaner and fresher the better
- At breaks get outside if possible

Music

- See page 79

RE-FOCUS

When you are ready to start learning re-focus

W hat's
I n
I t
F or
M e

'Why am I learning?'

COMMITTING

COMMITTING

STARTING FROM SCRATCH?
BEFORE BEGINNING TO STUDY

● Write down key headings/words that you already know, or use a Mind Map

This provides the links for the new information.

In the unlikely event you know absolutely nothing:

● Read the appropriate section of an encyclopedia

     or

● Read a book aimed at children; these are especially good as they are simple and have plenty of pictures to stimulate the right brain too

COMMITTING

THE 6 W'S
BEFORE BEGINNING TO STUDY

Create an interest in the material to be learned.

Remember - interest creates motivation to learn and aids retention.

Ask questions that you want answered by your study.

W ho?	Who discovered this? Who are the key characters?
W hat?	What are the counter arguments? What are the key facts?
W hen?	When was this discovered? When did this happen?
W here?	Where did this happen? Where was he/she born?
W hy?	Why did this happen? Why should I believe this?
Ho **W**?	How will this work? How does this relate to my existing knowledge?

If you are not asking questions you are not learning.

LEARNING STYLES

THREE KINDS OF MEMORY

Visual

- Visual learners find it easier to take in new information through pictures, diagrams, charts, films, etc

Auditory

- Verbal learners find it easier to take in new information through the spoken word

Kinaesthetic

- Kinaesthetic learners find it easier to take in new information through copying demonstrations and getting physically involved

Controlled by the Neocortex, see page 4.

COMMITTING

LEARNING STYLES
THREE KINDS OF MEMORY

The best learning takes place using all 3 memories, eg:

If you are reading:
- Visualise the key messages
- Read aloud or hear the words internally
- Get physically involved - underline, highlight, Mind Map, etc

Use all 3 styles (visual, auditory, kinaesthetic) to **V.A.K.** up knowledge.

Learners dominate in one style and have a preference for another.

Previous learning may have been hindered if it did not cater for your learning style. (Typically, schools are not geared to kinaesthetic learners.)

Assess where you dominate on the following pages, putting a tick in the box ☑, and use your preferred style to learn, using the following tips.

LEARNING STYLES
VISUAL LEARNERS

☐ Use phrases such as 'I **see** what you mean', 'I get the **picture**', 'That **looks** right'

☐ When relaxing, prefer to watch a film or video, go to the theatre or read a book

☐ Prefer to talk to people face to face

☐ Fast talkers, dislike listening to others

☐ Forget names, remember faces

☐ If lost or need directions, prefer a map

☐ When inactive, tend to doodle or watch someone/something

☐ When angry, are silent and seethe

☐ Reward people with a note, letter or card

☐ Well dressed, tidy and organised

COMMITTING

LEARNING STYLES
VISUAL LEARNERS

Learn best by:

- Writing down key facts or, better still, Mind Map
- Visualising what they are learning
- Creating pictures/diagrams from what they are learning
- Using time lines, for remembering dates
- Creating their own strong visual links
- Using pictures, diagrams, charts, film, video, graphics, etc

LEARNING STYLES
AUDITORY LEARNERS

- [ ] Use phrases such as
  'That **sounds** right', 'I **hear** what you are saying', 'That **rings** a bell'
- [ ] When relaxing, prefer to listen to music or radio
- [ ] Prefer to talk to people on the phone
- [ ] Enjoy listening to others, but impatient to talk; talk in a rhythmic voice
- [ ] Forget faces, remember names
- [ ] If lost or need directions, prefer to be told
- [ ] When inactive, tend to talk to themselves or others
- [ ] When angry, express themselves in outbursts
- [ ] Reward people with oral praise
- [ ] Do not like reading books or instruction manuals

LEARNING STYLES
AUDITORY LEARNERS

Learn best by:

- Hearing a seminar, presentation or explanation
- Reading aloud to themselves
- Reading with emotion or accent
- Making a tape of key points to listen to in the car, whilst ironing, etc
- Verbally summarise in their own words
- Explain the subject to someone else
- Use their own internal voice to verbalise what they are learning

COMMITTING

LEARNING STYLES
KINAESTHETIC LEARNERS

- [ ] Use phrases such as 'That **feels** right', 'I found it easy to **handle**', 'That **touched** a nerve'
- [ ] When relaxing, prefer to play games and sport
- [ ] Prefer to talk to people whilst doing something else
- [ ] Slow talkers, use gestures and expressions
- [ ] Shake hands with people they meet
- [ ] If lost or need directions, prefer to be shown the way
- [ ] When inactive, fidget
- [ ] When angry, clench their fists, grit their teeth and storm off
- [ ] Reward people with a pat on the back
- [ ] Cannot sit still for long periods of time

LEARNING STYLES
KINAESTHETIC LEARNERS

Learn best by:

- Copying demonstrations
- Making models
- Recording information as they hear it, preferably in a Mind Map
- Walking around, whilst they read
- Underlining/highlighting new information/key points
- Putting key points on to index cards and sorting them into order
- Getting physically and actively involved in their learning

SEVEN INTELLIGENCES

 Linguistic Intelligence - used for reading, writing and speech

Logical Mathematical Intelligence - used for Maths, logic and systems $\sqrt{8^2}$

 Visual Spacial Intelligence - used for visualisation and art

Musical Intelligence - used for rhythm, music and lyrics

 Bodily Kinaesthetic Intelligence - used for touch and reflex

Interpersonal Intelligence - used for communicating with others

 Intrapersonal Intelligence - used for self discovery and self analysis

The following pages on the 7 intelligences are based on and adapted from research by Howard Gardner & Colleagues at Harvard University.

SEVEN INTELLIGENCES

Everyone possesses all 7 intelligences to some extent.

The most powerful learning combines all 7.

They are all of value. You need to identify where your strengths lie and use those intelligences.

Assess your strengths on the following pages ☑ and use them by combining the different learning techniques.

SEVEN INTELLIGENCES
LINGUISTIC INTELLIGENCE

- **Used for reading, writing and speech**

Characteristics:

- ☐ Extensive vocabulary
- ☐ Good at spelling
- ☐ Good verbal and/or written communication
- ☐ Expressive fluent talker
- ☐ Good listener
- ☐ Gives clear explanations
- ☐ Reasoning ability
- ☐ Methodical

Likes:

- ☐ Reading
- ☐ Books
- ☐ Word games/crosswords
- ☐ Theatre
- ☐ Poetry
- ☐ Debate
- ☐ Radio
- ☐ Writing letters

COMMITTING

SEVEN INTELLIGENCES
LINGUISTIC INTELLIGENCE

Learning techniques:

- Learn from books, tapes, lectures, presentations, seminars, etc
- Write down questions you want answered before starting any learning
- Read out loud
- After reading a piece of text, summarise in your own words out loud and write it down
- Always put things into your own words
- Brainstorm to organise thoughts into order and/or key points
- Write key points on cards and sort into order
- Make up crosswords and puzzles to solve (why not do this with your learning set?)
- Debate and discuss issues (preferably with your learning set)
- Present what you have learned orally or in writing to someone else (your learning set?)

SEVEN INTELLIGENCES
LOGICAL MATHEMATICAL INTELLIGENCE

$$\sqrt{8^2}$$

- **Used for Maths, logic and systems**

Characteristics:

- [ ] Good at budgeting
- [ ] Logical thought, explanation and action
- [ ] Organised
- [ ] Organises tasks into sequence
- [ ] Plans time effectively
- [ ] Reasoning ability
- [ ] Seeks patterns and relationships
- [ ] Precise
- [ ] Good at planning journeys

Likes:

- [ ] Calculations, eg: dart scores, gambling odds, etc
- [ ] Solving puzzles
- [ ] Abstract thought
- [ ] Experimenting
- [ ] Science
- [ ] Computers

COMMITTING

SEVEN INTELLIGENCES
LOGICAL MATHEMATICAL INTELLIGENCE

$$\sqrt{8^2}$$

Learning techniques:

- List key points in order and number them
- Use a flow chart to express information/knowledge in easy to follow steps
- Use Mind Maps
- Use computers, eg: spreadsheets
- Experiment with the knowledge
- Use timelines for remembering dates and events
- Analyse and interpret data
- Use your reasoning and deductive skills
- Create and solve problems (this can be done with your learning set)
- Play mathematical games (this can be done with your learning set)

SEVEN INTELLIGENCES
VISUAL SPACIAL INTELLIGENCE

● **Used for visualisation and art**

Characteristics:

- ☐ Thinks and remembers in pictures
- ☐ Good sense of imaging/use of mind's eye
- ☐ Sense of colour
- ☐ Good at art/drawing
- ☐ Uses maps, charts and diagrams easily
- ☐ Sense of direction
- ☐ Good at driving/parking
- ☐ Well dressed

Likes

- ☐ Film and video
- ☐ Posters/pictures
- ☐ Drawing, painting, sculpting
- ☐ Doodling
- ☐ Colour
- ☐ Dressmaking
- ☐ Clothes
- ☐ Self assembly furniture
- ☐ Navigating
- ☐ Photography

SEVEN INTELLIGENCES
VISUAL SPACIAL INTELLIGENCE

Learning techniques:

- Learn from film, video, slides, etc
- Use symbols, doodles, diagrams or, better still, Mind Map
- Design and produce a poster of the key facts and pin it up
- Highlight key points with different colours
- When you read, visualise events in your mind's eye; do not focus on the words
- Use visualisation to create a mental TV documentary with strong visual images
- Study in different places/areas of a room to gain a different perspective
- Convert information into diagrams or cartoons

SEVEN INTELLIGENCES
MUSICAL INTELLIGENCE

- **Used for rhythm, music and lyrics**

Characteristics:

- [ ] Sensitive to pitch, rhythm and timbre
- [ ] Sensitive to emotion of music
- [ ] Changes mood with music
- [ ] Good at clapping in time to music
- [ ] Moves in time to music
- [ ] Remembers and repeats slogans and lyrics easily
- [ ] Good at selecting background music
- [ ] May be deeply spiritual

Likes:

- [ ] Radio
- [ ] Concerts
- [ ] Record collection
- [ ] Making music - plays an instrument
- [ ] Singing - in a choir or group
- [ ] Writing songs and/or music
- [ ] 'Working out' to music
- [ ] Relaxing to music

COMMITTING

SEVEN INTELLIGENCES
MUSICAL INTELLIGENCE

Learning techniques:

- Use music to relax before learning
- Study to music that represents what you are learning
- Study to Baroque music (see page 79)
- Read rhythmically (use a metronome)
- Write a song, jingle, rap, poem, rhyme, etc, to summarise key points

SEVEN INTELLIGENCES
BODILY KINAESTHETIC INTELLIGENCE

- **Used for touch and reflex**

Characteristics:

- [ ] Never sits still
- [ ] Fidgets
- [ ] Mechanically minded
- [ ] Likes to touch
- [ ] Solves problems physically 'hands on'
- [ ] Good with their hands
- [ ] Controlled reflexes
- [ ] Control of body
- [ ] Control of objects
- [ ] Good timing

Likes:

- [ ] Sport/games
- [ ] Rough and tumble play with children
- [ ] Acting/drama
- [ ] Dancing
- [ ] Cooking/baking
- [ ] Handicrafts
- [ ] D.I.Y.
- [ ] Car maintenance

COMMITTING

SEVEN INTELLIGENCES
BODILY KINAESTHETIC INTELLIGENCE

Learning techniques:

- Learn from what you do
- Use roleplay/drama to act out what you are learning
- Use field trips
- Get involved in the subject physically
- Take action - write down key points or, better still, Mind Map
- Make models
- Write key points on to index cards and sort them into order/groups and/or pin them up in your study area
- Move about whilst you are learning
- Change activity often and take frequent breaks
- Mentally review your learning whilst jogging/swimming/walking, etc

SEVEN INTELLIGENCES
INTERPERSONAL INTELLIGENCE

● **Used for communicating with others**

Characteristics:

- ☐ Relates to and mixes well with others
- ☐ Puts people at ease
- ☐ Has numerous friends
- ☐ Sympathetic to others' feelings
- ☐ Mediates between people in dispute
- ☐ Good communicator
- ☐ Good at negotiating
- ☐ Co-operative

Likes:

- ☐ Being with people
- ☐ Parties and social events
- ☐ Community activities
- ☐ Clubs
- ☐ Committee work
- ☐ Group activities/team tasks
- ☐ Managing/supervising
- ☐ Teaching/training
- ☐ Parenting

SEVEN INTELLIGENCES
INTERPERSONAL INTELLIGENCE

Learning techniques:

- Learn from others
- Work in teams and learn together
- Talk to others to get and share answers
- Compare notes after a study session
- Make use of networking and mentoring
- Teach others
- Socialise during breaks
- Form and learn through a learning set
- Throw a party to celebrate/reward your success

SEVEN INTELLIGENCES
INTRAPERSONAL INTELLIGENCE

- **Used for self discovery and self analysis**

Characteristics:

- [ ] Understands own feelings and behaviour
- [ ] Self intuitive, knows own strengths
- [ ] Private
- [ ] Independent
- [ ] Wants to be different from 'the crowd'
- [ ] Keeps a diary/journal
- [ ] Plans time effectively
- [ ] Self motivates
- [ ] Sets and achieves goals

Likes:

- [ ] Peace and quiet
- [ ] Daydreaming
- [ ] Reflecting/reminiscing
- [ ] Independence
- [ ] Achieving goals
- [ ] Own company

SEVEN INTELLIGENCES
INTRAPERSONAL INTELLIGENCE

Learning techniques:

- Use personal affirmations (see page 15)
- Set and achieve goals/targets with your learning
- Create personal interest, why does the subject matter to you
- Get interested, involved and motivated with the arguments and main characters
- Take control of your learning
- Carry out independent study
- Seek out background information, especially the human interest angle
- Listen to your intuition
- Reflect, write or discuss what you experienced and how you felt
- Reflect on how the information fits in with your existing knowledge and experiences

COMMITTING

POWER READING
PREPARATION

- Start with introductory text such as an encycledia or children's book
- Find the 3 best books in your area of interest (ask for referrals)
- List key headings of existing knowledge or Mind Map it
- Define your questions - the 6 W's (see page 31) so you read with a sense of interest
- Browse through each book casually and rapidly to identify:
  - organisation and structure
  - diagrams/pictures
  - appendices
  - preface
  - contents, etc
- Be selective, do not go further if it does not add to your existing knowledge
- Organise your reading into chunks (salami method)
- When you take breaks:
  - cup and uncup your hands over your eyes
  - focus on distant objects
  - do not rub your eyes

POWER READING
HOW TO READ

- Scan read for ideas and principles, not individual words
- Read the text; concentrate on beginning and end of paragraphs and chapters, or wherever else you identify key ideas are communicated
- Mark pages, highlight, underline, make notes, use codes as you go
- Skip over difficult text, return to it later when you have the full picture
- Read difficult text aloud
- Make key notes or Mind Map at the **end** of each chapter
- Review your notes/Mind Map
- Summarise the whole book in a few key notes/master Mind Map

Remember to celebrate your success and reward yourself.

POWER READING
PRINCIPLES

- Do not be afraid to disregard the book at any stage

- Never feel obliged to read a book from cover to cover

- Be flexible; adapt your reading to individual style
  of books/material - identify the style when you browse

- Read a book as you would a newspaper;
  only read the bits you want to,
  take control of your learning

COMMITTING

POWER READING

Try this simple test - answer all questions:

1 What is your favourite book?
2 Which spelling is correct : feasability or feasibility?
3 What was your favourite subject at school?
4 Work out what X is → 2 x X + 3 = 15
5 What did you have for breakfast?
6 Write your name backwards
7 What is your favourite film?
8 Repeat question 5
9 Ignore all the questions. If you answered, then see 10 below, if not turn the page
10 Re-read 'Power Reading', time spent now may save time in the future

COMMITTING

LEARNING SET

The ideal group is 2 - 6 people

Reasoning
- Establish a working contract for learning together
- Define the common objective and goal

Planning
- Break the learning into sections and assign to the set members
- Complete a learning plan

Committing
- Support each other, share opinions, experiences, knowledge and fears
- Use individual's strengths, especially learning styles

Reflecting
- Present your section to the set, proves if you know the subject
- Review how the set worked, to improve for the future
- Keep the set together for future learning projects
- Compete with other learning sets

COMMITTING

LEARNING SET
THE BENEFITS

- Makes learning fun and enjoyable
- Enjoy the mutual support of your set
- Saves time, as you will not have to research the whole subject
- Mixing learning styles ensures better learning
- Gain different opinions and viewpoints
- Raises the quality of your work
- You are committed if you are participating and contributing
- You will also learn how to work as a group, communicate and present your ideas
- Learning is improved - 2 heads are better than 1

COMMITTING

ON COURSE TECHNIQUES

Preparation	● Complete any required pre-course study
	● If there is none, gain a basic understanding of the subject
	● Bring any necessary books, literature, study aids, pens, paper, calculator, glasses, etc
Questions	● Prepare questions, know what you want to achieve
	● Use the 6 W's
Seating	● Front and centre; you are more involved, with fewer distractions between you and the trainer
	● Visual aids are easier to see, speech is easier to hear
	● Watch your posture; sit upright and attentive
Trainer	● The message is important, not the messenger
	● Listen to the message, ignoring irritating mannerisms
	● If you have done your preparation and prepared questions this will be easier

COMMITTING

ON COURSE TECHNIQUES

Listen	• Imagine the trainer is talking to you personally • Do not read, or ask colleagues to explain, during a session • If you have missed a point ask the trainer • Listen for key points
Notes	• Mind Map the key points; this will free up your time to listen
Learning style	• Use your own personal learning style • If not possible during a session, you must do some post course work
Breaks	• If you can, go outside for fresh air and a walk (especially at lunchtime) • Do not drink coffee and do not discuss what you are learning (let your subconscious process it)
Colleagues	• At the end of the day or course share your learning; you will gain a different perspective on the learning, and be surprised at what you have missed
Review/ Consolidate	• At the end of the day or course review your learning • Keep it current and fresh

MEMORY
WHAT IS MEMORY?

Consists of 3 stages:

Registration ● You get information

Retention ● You file information, which has the potential to be retrieved

Retrieval ● You find the information at some later stage when you need it

● Retrieval consists of:
 — **Recall:** voluntarily or involuntarily return the information to consciousness
 — **Recognition:** you cannot recall the information but you recognise it when you see it

'Retention' is not the problem, 'retrieval' is.

COMMITTING

MEMORY

RETENTION AND RETRIEVAL

Retention - you file information, which has the **potential** to be retrieved:

Hypnosis
- Under hypnosis people have recalled 'forgotten' memories and events perfectly

Near death experiences
- 'My *whole* life flashed before my eyes'
- Emotion is closely linked to memory
- Whilst highly emotive events are memorable, they also stimulate old memories

Surprise random recall
- 'Déjà vu'
- Stimulation of the senses can bring about recall of 'forgotten' memories and events
- A certain smell or taste brings it all back

Dreams
- Vivid dreams recalling 'forgotten' memories and events

Turn the page and write down everything you can remember from this page. Then turn back to check it against this page. The fact that you recognise this page means you have experienced 'recognition'. The trick is to master **voluntary** 'recall'.

MEMORY
HOW IT WORKS

There are 3 types of memory:

- Immediate (sensory) memory - Seconds

- Short term memory - Hours or days

- Long term memory - Months or years

MEMORY

SENSORY MEMORY TO LONG TERM MEMORY

- Learning involves getting information from sensory memory into the long term memory

- Anything in sensory memory can get in to the long term memory through **learning**

- Long term memory has no known storage limit

- When people talk about 'memory' they usually mean voluntary **retrieval** from long term memory

MEMORY

TEST

Read the following list of words, slowly, once. Then cover them up and answer the questions that follow.

HAND
CASE
ME
CAR
BOOK
AND
BRAIN
ME
HERE
TREE
MISSISSIPPI
OF
DOOR
AND
MUSIC
ME
HOME
FILM
WHITE
AND

COMMITTING

MEMORY

TEST

* How many of the first 5 words can you recall? ....

* How many of the last 5 words can you recall? ....

* Can you recall any words that appeared more
  than once? ....

* Was there any word which was outstandingly
  different from the rest? ....

* How many words can you recall that have something
  to do with what you have already read? ....

* How many of the words from the middle of the
  list, that you have not already noted above, can
  you recall? ....

Read on to check your results.

(69)

MEMORY
LEARNING WITHOUT BREAKS

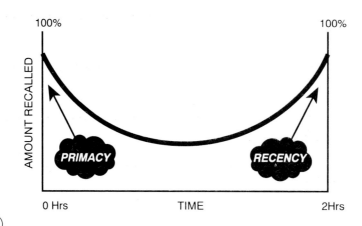

COMMITTING

MEMORY
LEARNING WITHOUT BREAKS

Primacy: • The start of a learning session is more memorable than the middle

1st events are more memorable

In the memory test you will have more easily recalled some first words

Recency: • The end of a learning session is more memorable than the middle

Recent events are more memorable

In the memory test you will have more easily recalled some last words

MEMORY
LEARNING WITH REGULAR BREAKS

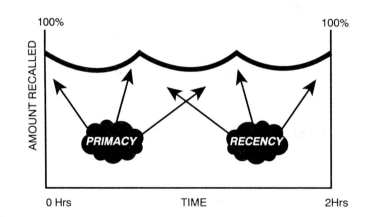

MEMORY
LEARNING WITH REGULAR BREAKS

- Keeps recall high, due to the increased effects of primacy and recency

- Increases as the subconscious processes the new information during breaks

- Relieves physical and mental tension

Ideal study time is 30 - 50 minutes.

Should be followed by a complete rest, from the type of study undertaken, of 5 - 10 minutes.

MEMORY
THE EFFECT OF LINKING

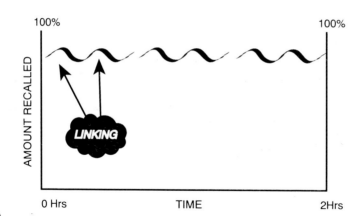

MEMORY
THE EFFECT OF LINKING

- You learn by linking new information to existing knowledge

- Recall occurs when the correct link is made and the information is found

- To aid linking, write down all you know about a subject before beginning any study, read introductory texts, etc

In the memory test you may have recalled 'BOOK', 'BRAIN' and/or 'MUSIC' as the words link to what you will have already read.

See page 78 for linking techniques.

MEMORY
THE EFFECT OF OUTSTANDINGNESS

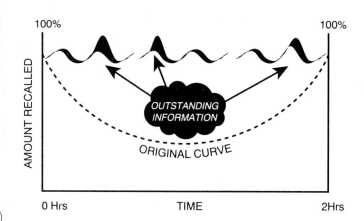

COMMITTING

MEMORY
THE EFFECT OF OUTSTANDINGNESS

You will recall unusual, outstanding, strange or absurd information more easily (known as the Von Restorff effect).

How often have you forgotten important appointments, names, statistics, etc? Yet you can still recall vividly something silly that occurred several years ago.

In the memory test you will have recalled 'MISSISSIPPI'.

COMMITTING

MEMORY
LINKING

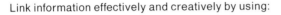

Link information effectively and creatively by using:

Outstandingness • Exaggerate size, shape, colour, movement and all of the following

Positive images • More likely to recall pleasant images

Humour • Funny events are more positive, outstanding and easier to recall

Sexuality • If you remember one of these 7 tips when you turn the page, this will be the one; most people remember well in this area

Sensuality • Make use of all the senses - see, hear, smell, touch and taste

Emotion • Emotive events are more memorable, use love, hate, fear, etc

Personality • There is no substitute for your own images and links; you are more likely to remember what you created
• Personal events and experiences are more memorable; involve yourself in your images

MUSIC

Certain types of music can match the body's rhythms, heartbeat, brainwaves, etc, inducing a state of relaxed alertness, for learning.

Baroque music, in particular, leaves the mind relaxed and open to learning. *(As pioneered by Dr Georgi Lozanov.)*

Experiment with music, to see what works best for you. If you find it distracting - do not use it.

MIND MAPS

BENEFITS

Mirrors how the brain looks and works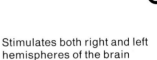

Makes use of linking

Makes use of different learning styles

Your ideas are easier to recall

Saves time, only recording and reviewing key words

Makes use of different intelligences

Stimulates both right and left hemispheres of the brain

Visual excitement aids memory

Easy to review, recreate from memory and check against original

$\sqrt{8^2}$

MIND MAPS
OTHER USES

- Training/Teaching
- Making a speech/presentation
- Project planning
- Writing reports/essays/books
- Brainstorming sessions
- Problem solving
- Creativity
- Taking minutes

MIND MAP MAXIMS

Paper

Good quality - stimulates all the senses
Blank - nothing to confine your creativity
Landscape - maximum space
Only use one side - easier to read

Central Image

Has more associations than a word and aids memory
Central image attracts the eye
Size 2" x 2", without frame
Use at least 4 colours, appealing - encourages learning

If you must use a word, use

DIMENSION and colour

MIND MAP MAXIMS

Branches

Main branches thicker, symbolise importance

Curved lines - stimulate visual interest

Length of line = length of word

Words

Only record key words

Main branch word - UPPER CASE

Secondary branches - lower case

ONE WORD PER LINE

Vary size relative to IMPORTANCE

Use for EMPHASIS

MIND MAP MAXIMS

Images

Stimulate the R - aid memory
Have more associations than words
Attract the eye, encourage learning
Eye takes in images faster than words
Where possible replace words with pictures

Colour

Stimulates the R - aids memory
Use one colour per main branch theme
Use for coding, enables faster access to information

MIND MAP MAXIMS

Codes

Use codes for instant linking of information, recurring themes and/or to save time

$- \times \div = \pm < > ° \bigcirc \bullet \triangle \nabla \star \blacklozenge \heartsuit \clubsuit \blacklozenge \spadesuit$

Use arrows to guide the eye to connecting themes

$\rightarrow \Rightarrow \blacktriangleright \Leftarrow \circlearrowright \leftrightarrows$

Spacing

Leave space

for CLARITY and ADD + ITIONS

MIND MAP MAXIMS

Personal style

Learning style is personal
Personal events are more memorable
Develop a personal style for your Mind Maps

Have fun

When learning is fun you learn faster and recall more
You are more likely to repeat the experience
It takes 72 muscles to frown and only 14 to smile

Relax and enjoy learning

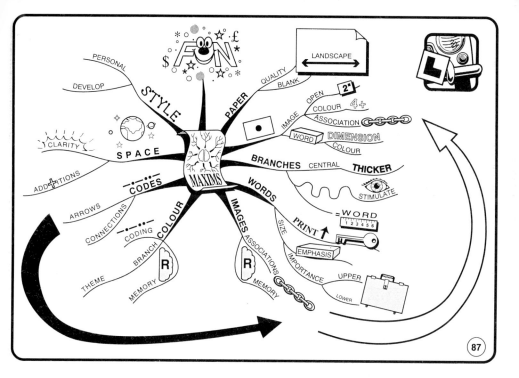

STYLE
PERSONAL
DEVELOP
FUN $ £

PAPER
QUALITY
BLANK
LANDSCAPE

IMAGE
OPEN 2"
COLOUR 4+
ASSOCIATION
WORD DIMENSION
COLOUR

SPACE
CLARITY
ADDITIONS

MAXIMS

BRANCHES
CENTRAL
THICKER
STIMULATE

CODES
ARROWS
CONNECTIONS
CODING
COLOUR
BRANCH R
THEME
MEMORY R

WORDS
= WORD
1 2 3 4 5 6
SIZE
PRINT
EMPHASIS
IMPORTANCE
UPPER
LOWER

IMAGES
ASSOCIATIONS
MEMORY R

87

REVIEW
WHY

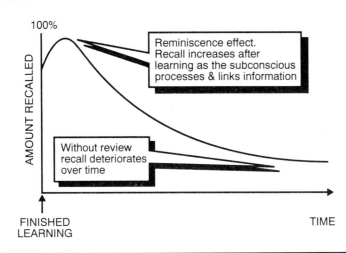

Reminiscence effect.
Recall increases after
learning as the subconscious
processes & links information

Without review
recall deteriorates
over time

100%

AMOUNT RECALLED

FINISHED
LEARNING

TIME

COMMITTING

REVIEW

WHY AND HOW

- Once you have learned something, it is easier to keep that knowledge fresh than to start again

- Do not let what you have learned go to waste

- Reviewing embeds that knowledge in your long term memory

- Repetition is not enough - **use a different learning method**
  - review Mind Maps by re-creating them
  - review only what you want to remember
  - key facts only
  - not everything you have read, heard, seen or done

REVIEW

WHEN

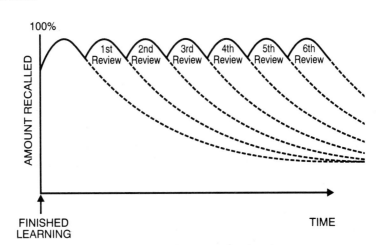

COMMITTING

REVIEW
WHEN

REVIEW	WHEN	HOW LONG
1st review	10-30 minutes after a learning event	For 5 minutes
2nd review	1 day after	For 5 minutes
3rd review	1 week after	For 5 minutes
4th review	1 month after	For 3 minutes
5th review	3 months after	For 3 minutes
6th review	6 months after	For 3 minutes

Stored in long term memory

COMMITTING

MENTORING

- A mentor is an individual skilled in the area you are learning

- They should be supportive and provide further information

- Watch them, talk to them, use their ideas and methods

- There should be a two way contract which is mutually beneficial to both parties - even if it is only buying lunch, whilst you pick their brains

- Return the favour to someone else by being a mentor yourself

REFLECTING

REFLECTING

TEST YOURSELF

Have you learned?

- Before testing yourself, set a standard and keep it

- Speed is not important - getting it right is

- Use, or create, mock exams

- Use mental rehearsal/visualisation

- Re-create Mind Maps from memory

- Teach others (your learning set) - this really proves if you know your stuff

- If you are learning to learn - learn something, put it to the test

TEST YOURSELF

If you learn to drive, you get in a car.
If you learn to swim, you jump in the water. So:

- If you are learning how to Mind Map - Mind Map books, TV, documentaries, etc
- If you are learning how to write - put pen to paper
- If you are learning French - parlez français
- If you are learning Chinese cookery - buy a wok and start using it
- If you are learning about computers - sit in front of one and use it
- If you are learning how to deliver speeches - stand up and talk
- If you are learning bookkeeping - get your calculator out
- If you are learning how to learn - learn something, use the techniques in this book

No child has learned to talk only by watching others and reading about it; sooner or later they open their mouths.

REFLECTING

LEARNING SET

Test yourselves:

- Present your learning to the set
- Test the set
  — set tests — run quizzes — have question and answer sessions
- Compete against other learning sets

Ask yourselves:

'What worked well?' 'What could we do better next time?'

Points to consider:

- contract
- openness
- competition
- quality of work
- support
- roles
- mix of styles
- benefits

What next?

REFLECTING

IMPROVING

'What worked well?'

'What could I do better next time?'

If you ask these questions and act on the answers, you will develop your learning ability.

It is as important to understand and repeat what did work well as it is to improve on anything that did not.

Remember - you are responsible for your own learning.

REFLECTING

REWARD

You should recognise and reward your successes.

- It encourages positive emotions about learning

- Ensures learning is fun, rewarding, enjoyable and worth doing again

- Incentives should be given along the way, but, in particular, at the end of a learning event

- All too often they are overlooked and any success passes unrecognised, never to be repeated

REWARD

The reward is not: having the knowledge, passing the exam, getting the qualification, achieving the promotion or the feeling that any of this gives you.

Reward is:

- Eating out at a special restaurant
- Having a weekend break
- Watching a show at a theatre
- Doing something unusual:
  - bungee jumping
  - driving a racing car
  - parachute jumping
  - water ski-ing, etc
- Sharing your success with others

How will you reward yourself for learning how to learn?

REWARD

Use this page to write down the reward you will give yourself when you have learnt how to learn.

MEMORY TRICKS

TECHNIQUES

Principles	-	Principles are easier to recall than individual examples, eg: 'I before E, except after C, or when sounded like A, as in neighbour or weigh'
Rhyme	-	Makes use of musical intelligence, eg: '30 days hath September ...'
Acronym	-	Forming a word from the first letter(s) of other words, eg: **H** uron **O** ntario **M** ichigan The great lakes **E** rie **S** uperior
Mnemonic	-	Generic term for any memory aid, eg: '**E**very **G**ood **B**oy **D**eserves **F**avour' **EGBDF,** the musical notes on the line of staff

NUMBERS

Numbers are traditionally hard to remember. They lack feeling, image, motion, humour and are, in comparison to a word, meaningless.

Use the following method to convert numbers to words and pictures, therefore making them easier to remember.

Number	Code	Remember
0	S, Z	first sound of the word 'zero'
1	T, D	both t and d have 1 downstroke
2	N	n has 2 downstrokes
3	M	m has 3 downstrokes
4	R	final sound of the word 'four'
5	L	roman numeral for 50, make L with your hand (5 digits)
6	J, CH, SH soft G	j turned around is like the number 6
7	K, hard C, hard G	k formed from two 7's, one reversed
8	F, V	f and 8 both have two loops, one above the other
9	P, B	p reversed is 9

MEMORY TRICKS

NUMBERS IN PRACTICE

This system can be used to remember any sequence of numbers, eg:

    123 = DNM   = **Denim**
    921210 = PNDNTS = **Pound notes**

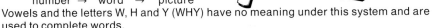

number → word → picture

Vowels and the letters W, H and Y (WHY) have no meaning under this system and are used to complete words.

What about the following?

    number → word → picture
    54226 = ? = ? *Answer at bottom of page*

Practise the system regularly, break numbers down into words for speed.

*Based on the work of Stanislaus Mink Von Wennsshein 1648 and
Dr Richard Grey 1730*

54226 = L R N N G = Learning

NUMBERS IN PRACTICE

The number system covered is worth learning; why not try the following method too,
eg:

Pi =   0.318310 .....

0. 3 1 8   3 10

Can I remember the reciprocal

The letters in each word total the number you want to remember.

What about our earlier number 5 4 2 2 6 ?

Suggestion at bottom of page

DATES

Try using the system covered earlier, on page 103.

Wall Street Crash   1929 - 2 = N,   9 = P
N a P   Picture yourself driving a car, having a nap and crashing into a wall

Chamberlain declares war on Germany   3/9/1939 - 3 = M,   9 = D
M a D M a D =   Picture a mad and angry Chamberlain fighting a mad and angry Hitler

And/or try a time line:

MEMORY TRICKS

NEW ANGLES

Try a different angle -

eg: The difference between a
Bactrian camel and a Dromedary camel

eg: Remembering the following 4 months

March   June   September   December

This time it is easier to use the numbers

3   6   9   12

as they have a meaning

MEMORY TRICKS

PEG SYSTEMS

- A method used for remembering lists/sequences

- You use a memorised sequence of hooks, on to which you link new information

For effective links, see Linking, page 78.

Make your peg system personal. Create your own words/images. Personal ideas are easier to recall.

The number system, on page 103, could be used as a peg system giving you thousands of pegs on to which you can link new information.

MEMORY TRICKS

PEG SYSTEMS

Number System

1	=	D	=	Day
2	=	N	=	Noah
3	=	M	=	May
4	=	R	=	Ray
5	=	L	=	Lay
6	=	J	=	Jay
7	=	K	=	Key
8	=	F	=	Fee
9	=	B	=	Bay
10	=	DZ	=	Daze

etc

Number Rhyme

1	=	Gun
2	=	Chew
3	=	Tree
4	=	Door
5	=	Hive
6	=	Bricks
7	=	Heaven
8	=	Gate
9	=	Wine
10	=	Hen

MEMORY TRICKS

PEG SYSTEMS
NUMBER SHAPE

1 = Pen

2 = Swan

3 = Hills

4 = Boat

5 = Hook

6 = Yo-Yo

7 = Boomerang

8 = Egg-timer

9 = Flag

10 = Bat & ball

MEMORY TRICKS

PEG SYSTEMS
ALPHABET SYSTEM

The peg word must start with the sound of the letter, eg:
A = **A**ce not **A**pple, C - **S**ea not **C**at.

A	=	Ace	J	=	Jay	S	=	Eskimo
B	=	Bee	K	=	Cake	T	=	Tea
C	=	Sea	L	=	Elbow	U	=	Yew
D	=	Deed	M	=	Empire	V	=	Venus
E	=	Easel	N	=	Enema	W	=	WC
F	=	Effluent	O	=	Obese	X	=	X-ray
G	=	Gee Gee	P	=	Pea	Y	=	Y-fronts
H	=	H-Bomb	Q	=	Queue	Z	=	Z car
I	=	Eye	R	=	Arm			

MEMORY TRICKS

PEG SYSTEMS
DAYS AND MONTHS

Days of the week

Sunday	-	sun
Monday	-	money
Tuesday	-	chew
Wednesday	-	wedding
Thursday	-	thirsty
Friday	-	fry
Saturday	-	saturn

Months of the year

January	-	New Year
February	-	Brewery
March	-	Marching
April	-	Ape
May	-	Maypole
June	-	Bride
July	-	Jewel
August	-	Gust
September	-	Sceptre
October	-	Octopus
November	-	Fireworks
December	-	Christmas

Use your own 'personal' images, more memorable.

BLOCKS TO LEARNING

BLOCKS TO LEARNING

WHAT ARE THEY?

Psychological	Wrong state of mind, negative attitude to learning, fear, etc
Physiological	Poor environment, distractions, too comfortable and relaxed
Learning style	Not knowing how you learn best
Time	Not having the time, learning solidly for hours, burning the midnight oil - especially prior to an exam
Subject	Lack of interest, lack of understanding
Experience	Previous bad experiences of learning

BLOCKS TO LEARNING

OVERCOMING BLOCKS TO LEARNING

Psychological   Use relaxation techniques to prepare for learning
and exercise regularly
Have a clear focus on why you are learning
Use positive affirmations and visualisation to reinforce success
Reward yourself, make learning fun and you are more likely to repeat the process
Use your learning set or mentor to support your fears and praise your success

Physiological   Prepare your environment for learning
Avoid distractions, such as noise, visual distractions and comfortable armchairs

Learning style   Find your strengths and use them to your advantage

OVERCOMING BLOCKS TO LEARNING

Time	Plan out your learning (use a learning plan)
	Prior to an exam, relax - don't cram. If you have used a learning plan, you should have completed all your learning
Subject	Have a clear focus on why you are learning
	Reward yourself
	Read simple introductory texts at first
	Prepare your questions (the 6 W's) and get involved
Experience	All of the above may have caused this experience
	Is it really as bad as you perceive or have you created it
	That is the past, you cannot change it - now is the time to move on

**"What we know today will be obsolete
tomorrow. If we stop learning we stagnate."**

Dorothy D Billington

Adults Who Learn and Grow *

*_Article in 'New Horizons for Learning' Spring 1993_

MASTER MIND MAP - LEARNING

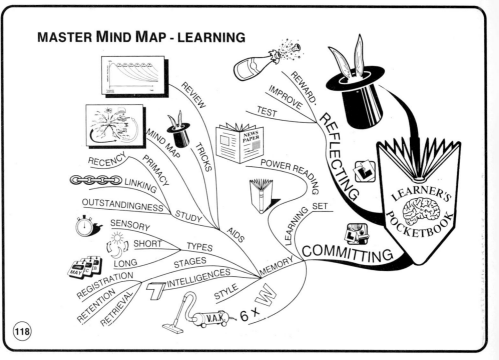

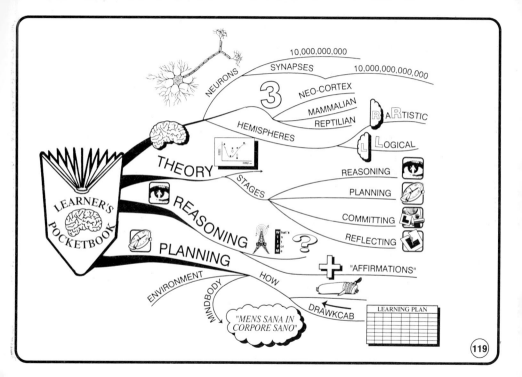

NEURONS 10,000,000,000

SYNAPSES 10,000,000,000,000

3 NEO-CORTEX

MAMMALIAN

REPTILIAN

HEMISPHERES

R ARTISTIC

L LOGICAL

THEORY

STAGES

REASONING

PLANNING

COMMITTING

REFLECTING

What's in it for Me WIIFM ?

REASONING

PLANNING

+ "AFFIRMATIONS"

ENVIRONMENT

HOW

MINDBODY

DRAWKCAB

LEARNING PLAN

"MENS SANA IN CORPORE SANO"

LEARNER'S POCKETBOOK

BIBLIOGRAPHY

'Make the Most of your Mind', Tony Buzan, Pan
'Use your Memory', Tony Buzan, BBC Books
'The Learning Revolution', Gordon Dryden & Dr Jeannette Vos, Profile
'Total Recall', John Minninger PhD, Thorsons
'Get Ahead', Vanda North & Tony Buzan, BBC Books
'Superlearning', Sheila Ostander & Lynn Schroeder, Souvenir Press
'Rapid Reading', Kathryn Redway, Pan
'Accelerated Learning', Colin Rose, Accelerated Learning Systems Ltd
'Accelerate Your Learning', Colin Rose & Louise Goll, Accelerated Learning
   Systems Ltd
'The Brain Book' Peter Russell, Routledge & Kegan Paul
'How to Boost your Brain Power', Roger B Yepsen, Jnr, Thorsons

About the Author

Paul Hayden AMIPD MLIA (dip) FPC began his training career at Allied Dunbar, where he had responsibility for the development of head office personnel and, later, the sales force.

As an independent training consultant, for clients which include Prudential, Businesslink, B.P.P. Publishing and the Chartered Insurance Institute, Paul has designed numerous training materials and developed individuals' potential using his specialist knowledge of learning.

He is the author of several in-house training manuals and co-author of 'The Financial Advisers Guide'.

Paul can be contacted through:
The Hayden Partnership, PO box 965, Swindon, Wiltshire, SN5 9YS.
Telephone 01793 879245

Published by Management Pocketbooks Ltd.

First published in 1995. Reprinted 1997

Printed in England by Alresford Press Ltd., Alresford, Hants. SO24 9QF

ORDER FORM

Please send me .... copies of 'The Learner's Pocketbook'

.... copies of ....Pocketbook

.... copies of ....Pocketbook

.... copies of ....Pocketbook

.... copies of ....Pocketbook

Title *(Mr/Mrs/Miss/Ms)* Forename

Surname

Position

Organisation

Address

Postcode

Telephone

Nature of Business

Complete and return to:

Melrose Film Productions Limited,
Dumbarton House, 68 Oxford Street, London W1N 0LH
Tel: 0171 627 8404   *Fax: 0171 622 0421*

MELROSE